DISCOVERING
CENTRAL AMERICA

Guatemala

DISCOVERING CENTRAL AMERICA

Guatemala

Charles J. Shields

Mason Crest Publishers
Philadelphia

Mason Crest Publishers
370 Reed Road
Broomall PA 19008
www.masoncrest.com

First printing

1 3 5 7 9 8 6 4 2

Library of Congress Cataloging-in-Publication Data
on file at the Library of Congress

ISBN 1-59084-095-X

**DISCOVERING
CENTRAL AMERICA**

Belize
Central America: Facts and Figures
Costa Rica
El Salvador

Guatemala
Honduras
Nicaragua
Panama

Discovering Central America

James D. Henderson

CENTRAL AMERICA is a beautiful part of the world, filled with generous and friendly people. It is also a region steeped in history, one of the first areas of the New World explored by Christopher Columbus. Central America is both close to the United States and strategically important to it. For nearly a century ships of the U.S. and the world have made good use of the Panama Canal. And for longer than that breakfast tables have been graced by the bananas and other tropical fruits that Central America produces in abundance.

Central America is closer to North America and other peoples of the world with each passing day. Globalized trade brings the region's products to world markets as never before. And there is promise that trade agreements will soon unite all nations of the Americas in a great common market. Meanwhile improved road and air links make it easy for visitors to reach Middle America. Central America's tropical flora and fauna are ever more accessible to foreign visitors having an interest in eco-tourism. Other visitors are drawn to the region's dazzling Pacific Ocean beaches, jewel-like scenery, and bustling towns and cities. And everywhere Central America's wonderful and varied peoples are outgoing and welcoming to foreign visitors.

These eight books are intended to provide complete, up-to-date information on the five countries historians call Central America (Guatemala, El Salvador, Honduras, Nicaragua, Costa Rica), as well as on Panama (technically part of South America) and Belize (technically part of North America). Each volume contains chapters on the land, history, economy, people, and cultures of the countries treated. And each country study is written in an engaging style, employing a vocabulary appropriate to young students.

A young Indian girl tends a small sheep herd alongside a road in Guatemala.

All volumes contain colorful illustrations, maps, and up-to-date boxed information of a statistical character, and each is accompanied by a chronology, a glossary, a bibliography, selected Internet resources, and an index. Students and teachers alike will welcome the many suggestions for individual and class projects and reports contained in each country study, and they will want to prepare the tasty traditional dishes described in each volume's recipe section.

This eight-book series is a timely and useful addition to the literature on Central America. It is designed not just to inform, but also to engage school-aged readers with this important and fascinating part of the Americas.

Let me introduce this series as author Charles J. Shields begins each volume: *¡Hola!* You are discovering Central America!

(Opposite) The cone of Volcan Agua rises over the city of Antigua. Guatemala is home to more than 30 volcanoes, including the highest one in Central America. (Right) Two people gaze up at a massive Ceiba tree near Tikal. The Ceiba, which can grow taller than 100 feet (31 meters) is the national tree of Guatemala.

1 The Country of Eternal Spring

¡HOLA! ARE YOU DISCOVERING Guatemala? Welcome to the place known as the Country of Eternal Spring, where the ruins of ancient temples poke above jungle vegetation, where volcanoes cast a red glow at night, and where handsome examples of colonial Spanish buildings contrast with modern architecture in the capital, Guatemala City. This is a land of adventure, only recently at peace after nearly 36 years of civil war.

A Jumble of Volcanoes and Jungle

In total area, Guatemala is about the size of Tennessee, a medium-size state. Bounded by Mexico to the north and west, the Pacific Ocean to the southwest, Belize and the Caribbean Sea to the east, and Honduras and El

Quick Facts: The Geography of Guatemala

Location: Central America, bordering the Caribbean Sea, between Honduras and Belize, and bordering the northern Pacific Ocean, between El Salvador and Mexico.

Geographic coordinates: 15'30"N, 90'15"W

Area: (slightly smaller than New York)
  total: 108,890 sq. km
  land: 108,430 sq. km
  water: 460 sq. km

Borders: Belize 266 km, El Salvador 203 km, Honduras 256 km, Mexico 962 km.

Terrain: mostly mountains with narrow coastal plains and rolling limestone plateaus.

Climate: tropical; hot, humid in lowlands; cooler in highlands.

Elevation extremes:
  lowest point: Pacific Ocean 0 m
  highest point: Volcan Tajumulco 4,211 m

Natural resources: petroleum, nickel, rare woods, fish, chicle (gum), hydropower.

Land use:
  arable land: 12 percent
  permanent crops: 5 percent
  permanent pastures: 24 percent
  forests and woodland: 54 percent
  other: 5 percent
  Irrigated land: 1,250 sq. km

Salvador to the southeast, Guatemala is Central America's westernmost country.

Guatemala's land has been described as a "mountainous and forested jumble of volcanoes and jungle." One-third of the country is mountainous and a nearly equal amount is covered by thick tropical forests.

The highlands are a chain of mountains running east to west across Guatemala. The high *plateau* and mountain systems in this region include the Sierra Madre, Sierra de Chaucus, Sierra de las Minas, Montanas del Mico, Sierra de los Chuchumatanes, and the Sierra de Chama. The highlands provide coffee- and corn-growing farmland, and it is also where most Guatemalans live, including the country's Indians. The highlands are dotted by the blackened cones of more than 30 volcanoes. The highest of these is Volcan Tajumulco, which at 13,816 feet (4,211 meters) is also the highest mountain in Central America. Six volcanoes have erupted with smoke and lava in recent years. Unfortunately, Guatemala is shaken by earthquakes, also. Twenty-three thousand people were killed, and 70,000 injured by an earthquake in Guatemala in 1976.

The volcano Pacaya emits steam and ash in October 2001. Pacaya is located in Escuintla, about 40 miles from Guatemala's capital. The active volcano is one of 36 that make up the Guatemalan volcanic chain.

Lush vegetation grows in the rainforest of Guatemala's interior lowlands. Tikal, once an important center of the Mayan culture, is located nearby.

The Northern Plain is the least populated and least developed area of Guatemala. Some hardwood trees covering the plain produce chicle, a gummy resin used in making chewing gum. Mahogany, cedar, and balsam trees can be found here, too, which are used in construction and furniture-making.

Thick rain forest dominates the interior lowland of El Petén, a rolling limestone plateau occupying part of the Yucatán Peninsula, where the deep, rich soil yields dinosaur bones and nourishes enormous banana plantations. Ancient Mayan cities, such as Tikal, can be found here, too. The Guatemalan jungle is home to rare creatures—jaguar, ocelot, puma, jaguarundi, and margay—in addition to the more commonly seen deer, peccary, tapir, and monkey. There are more than 900 species of birds in Guatemala, 204 species of reptiles, and 8,000 species of plants.

The Pacific Lowland coast features *lagoons* and a tropical *savanna* plain, which is intensively farmed. Rivers and streams flowing through the Pacific Lowland make it ideal for sugar cane and cotton plantations, cattle ranches, and farms that grow corn and beans. The Pacific coastline itself is a winding ribbon of mostly rather rough black-sand beaches. The tiny Caribbean coastline in the Bay of Honduras lacks beaches, but culturally it has much to offer. The *Continental Divide* and Caribbean Lowlands contain three deep river valleys—the Motagua, Polochic, and Sarstun.

Overall, 18 short rivers flow through Guatemala from the high plateaus to the Pacific Ocean. There are also four major lakes: Lake Atitlán, Lake Amatitlán, Lake Petén Itza, and Lake Izabel, the country's largest lake at 228 square miles (591 sq. km).

Environmental Challenges

Deforestation, poor water use, and pollution are serious problems affecting Guatemala. Over 50 percent of the forests have been destroyed since 1890, causing soil erosion and threatening the existence of many endangered species, including Guatemala's gorgeous national bird, the quetzál. In addition, nearly three-quarters of the country's water is used for agriculture, leaving 57 percent of the people in rural areas without pure drinking water. Instead they rely on catching rainwater, or carrying water from sources they can find.

Solid waste from the cities, as well as the heavy use of chemical soil fertilizers, contributes strongly to pollution. Guatemala's major cities are Guatemala City (population 2,697,000), the largest city in Central America; Mixco (population 436,700); Villa Nueva (population 165,600); Chinautla

A malachite butterfly pauses on a leaf in the El Petén rainforest. The Guatemalan rainforest is home to thousands of different types of birds, animals, and plants. Sadly, many of these are endangered by the continued destruction of the rainforest.

(population 61,300); and Amatitlán (population 40,200). Studies by the United Nations show that a large number of respiratory and digestive illnesses suffered by Guatemalans are the result of environmental contamination.

A Tropical Climate

In general, Guatemala has a tropical climate. However, the highland elevations at which most Guatemalans live—between 3,000 and 8,000 feet (915 and 2,440 m) above sea level—are regions where the days are warm and the nights are cool. The higher valleys even have frost at times. The average annual temperature is 68° F (20° C).

Temperatures in the highlands change with the seasons. Guatemala has two primary seasons—the wet season, from May to October, and the dry season, from November to May. During the wet season, the highlands are cold at night and damp and chilly during the day. The weather turns sunny and pleasant during the dry season. Guatemala City, where one-eighth of the population lives, has average annual temperatures of 54° to 73° F (12° to 23° C) in January and 61° to 84° F (16° to 29° C) in May.

The climate throughout the El Petén lowlands varies from hot and humid (tropical) to hot and dry (arid). The same is true of both the Caribbean and Pacific coasts. Temperatures along the Pacific coast can be sweltering, hovering around 100° F (38° C) for parts of the year.

The Pacific lowlands and western highlands receive 30 to 60 inches (76 to 150 cm) of rain a year; the eastern highlands gets 20 to 30 inches (51 to 76 cm). The city of Guatemala, in the southern highlands, receives about 52 inches (about 132 cm) of rain annually. During the wet season, rain falls almost daily. In the Northern Plain, where rain falls most of the year, annual amounts total between 80 and 150 inches (200 to 381 cm).

Occasionally, a hurricane hits Guatemala. On October 25, 1998, Hurricane Mitch, the fourth most intense Atlantic Ocean hurricane on record, slammed into the Central American coastline. At its height on October 26 and 27, Hurricane Mitch sustained winds of 180 mph and triggered four days of constant heavy rains, causing damage in the billions of dollars to Honduras, Guatemala, Nicaragua, and El Salvador.

(Opposite) Visitors to Guatemala climb the steps of a Mayan temple in Tikal. The Maya built a complex civilization in Central America more than 1,100 years ago. (Right) La Merced, a church in Antigua, provides a striking example of Spanish colonial architecture. Antigua was at the center of Spanish power in the region during the 16th and 17th centuries.

2 A National Identity Marred by Conflict

GUATEMALA WAS HOME to the Maya, who built a great ancient civilization in the Western hemisphere. Beginning in the mid-16th century, though, Spanish *colonial* rule initiated centuries of oppression against the native people. Not until the mid-20th century did *reform*-minded leaders try to undo the injustices of the past. By then, however, internal anger had reached a peak, eventually sparking a long and violent civil war.

A Lost Civilization, Colonial Rule, and Religion

More than half of all Guatemalans are descendants of native Mayan nations, which emerged from the fishing and farming villages along the country's Pacific coast as early as 2000 B.C. The people in these villages were

17

Did You Know?

- Guatemala's flag has a white vertical stripe between two blue vertical stripes, with the coat of arms centered in the white band.
- The national bird is the quetzál, the symbol of love and liberty, which, according to legend, dies if placed in captivity.
- The national flower is the white nun, a member of the orchid family.

the forerunners of a great civilization in Central America. Today, only hilltop ruins remain of the great Mayan temples that were beginning to appear in the highlands by A.D. 250.

The center of Mayan power moved from the north to the El Petén interior lowlands between A.D. 600 and 900 to consolidate authority in one location. Then, for reasons unclear to historians, the Mayan civilization suddenly declined in 900. Another native people, the Itzaes also settled in El Petén. When Pedro de Alvarado came to claim Guatemala on behalf of Spain in 1523, he found the native tribes at war. The Spanish armies crushed these tribes, as well as the remaining highland kingdoms of the Quiché and Cakchiquel Maya. The Catholic Church sent Dominican, Franciscan, and Augustinian friars to *convert* the conquered people to Christianity. During the centuries of Spanish colonial rule that followed, the importance of the Mayan culture was largely forgotten and destroyed.

Today, Roman Catholicism is practiced by a majority of Guatemalans, though some native people add to it traditional Mayan forms of religion, such as ancestor worship and praying to the forces of nature. Westernized Mayans and *mestizos* (mixed non-Indian and native ancestry) are known as Ladinos. Protestant Christianity is practiced by 10 percent of the population, and the Mayan religion by 30 percent. The official language of

Guatemala is Spanish, but not all of the people descended from the Maya understand it. After decades of conflict between the government and rebel groups from the countryside, the Peace Accords, signed in 1996, provide in part for the translation of some official documents and voting materials into several Mayan languages.

Three Capitals

During the three centuries of Spanish colonial rule, Guatemala had three capital cities. The first two were destroyed by natural disasters. Floods and an earthquake buried the original colonial capital, Ciudad Vieja, in 1542. Survivors founded the second capital, Antigua, in 1543, which become one of the richest cities in the world during the 17th century. Then, after two disastrous earthquakes in 1773, Guatemalans abandoned Antigua to build the third capital, Guatemala City, in 1776. In the old capital of Antigua, examples of Spanish architecture have been preserved as national monuments.

Guatemala declared independence from Spain for all of Central America in 1821. For a time, Guatemala became part of the Mexican empire. Then it joined a federation called the United Provinces of Central America. Despite this declaration of freedom, people living in the country who were of Spanish descent, or of mixed Spanish and native blood (*mestizos*), held most of the power. The native people were unprotected by the law, and saw huge tracts of their land seized and turned into plantations for raising tobacco and sugar cane. Forced to work the land for the new owners, their condition was not much better than slavery. From the mid-nineteenth century to the mid-twentieth, Guatemala was governed by either harsh dictators or by leaders who were more interested in promoting business interests than helping the people.

Reform Followed by Repression

In 1945, following the overthrow of a military dictator, *civilian* president Juan José Arévalo came to power. Arévalo established the nation's social security and health systems and a government bureau to look after Mayan concerns. His *regime* withstood 25 takeover attempts by the military between 1945 and 1951. Reforms put in place by Arévalo were continued by his successor, Colonel Jacobo Arbenz Guzmán. But Guzmán's efforts to break up large estates and to take control of lands dominated by foreign companies—including the United Fruit Company headquartered in the United States—and his encouragement of the Communist Party led to his downfall. The army refused to defend him when the United States Central Intelligence Agency (CIA) helped organize an overthrow. In 1954, Colonel Carlos Castillo Armas invaded the country from Honduras with assistance from the United States and Guzmán fled to Mexico.

Guatemala was then ruled by *repressive* military-led governments. Armed rebels, directed from Communist Cuba beginning in 1960, waged guerrilla war against the government, a conflict that would continue for 36 years. Four principal *left-wing* guerrilla groups—the Guerrilla Army of the Poor (EGP), the Revolutionary Organization of Armed People (ORPA), the Rebel Armed Forces (FAR), and the Guatemalan Labor Party (PGT)— targeted business and government buildings and fought security forces.

Following a strong counterstrike by the military in the countryside, the guerrillas then concentrated their attacks in Guatemala City, where they assassinated leading figures, including U.S. Ambassador John Gordon Mein in 1968. Extreme *right-wing* groups of self-appointed *vigilantes*, including the Secret Anti-Communist Army (ESA) and the White Hand, tortured and murdered students, professionals, and peasants suspected of involvement in guerrilla activities. Catholic priests working in rural areas became activists, leading campaigns for social justice, sometimes at the cost of their lives. On July 18, 1982, General Rios Montt, the president of Guatemala, was quoted in the *New York Times* as telling an audience of native Guatemalans, "If you are with us, we'll feed you; if not, we'll kill you." Under Rios Montt and others, thousands died at the hands of secret death squads.

A Halt to the Killing

Americans became more aware of the violence in Guatemala as a result of news reporting and with the 1983 publication of *I, Rigoberta Menchú, An Indian Woman in Guatemala*. This book soon became assigned reading in college courses about Central America. Finally, the violence against anti-government forces led the United States to cut off

Rigoberta Menchú's autobiography provided a graphic look at the violence in Guatemala. She has continued working as an advocate for human rights, both in Guatemala and throughout Central America, and received the Nobel Peace Prize for her efforts.

military aid to Guatemala. The Guatemalan Congress drafted a new, more democratic constitution, which led to the 1985 election of the civilian president Marco Vinicio Cerezo Arévalo, a relative of the earlier reform president, Juan José Arévalo. President Cerezo's civilian government pledged that its top priorities would be to end the political violence and to establish the rule of law.

Nevertheless, the government failed to deal with human rights issues, such as poverty, illiteracy, infant mortality, inadequate health and social services, and rising levels of violence. This set off a new round of national protests. Following a series of shake-ups in the government and another overhaul of the constitution in 1993, government leaders signed a series of Peace Accords with *leftist guerrillas* in December 1996, and the army

Three residents of Puerto Barrios pull their boat through the high water on the city's streets in October 1998. The flooding was caused by Hurricane Mitch, which hit Guatemala with devastating force, killing hundreds of people and causing billions of dollars worth of damage.

Guatemala's president, Alfonso Portillo, meets with U.S. President George W. Bush at the White House in July 2001. The two leaders discussed regional issues. Portillo has attempted to continue the peace process and work toward ensuring human rights in Guatemala.

agreed to reduce its role in policing the country. Currently, foreign aid and charity groups have made carrying out the Peace Accords a condition of continuing to help in Guatemala. However, the lopsidedness of wealth and influence, favoring those of Spanish descent, still remains a constant challenge to peace in Guatemala.

Guatemala swore in a new government on January 14, 2000, under its recently elected president, Alfonso Portillo, who won with two-thirds of the popular vote. Portillo promised during his campaign to continue the peace process, appoint a civilian defense minister, reform the armed forces, replace the military secret service with a civilian one, and strengthen the protection of human rights.

(Opposite) A man taps a rubber tree to start the sap running into the collection cup. Natural rubber has been an important export crop for many years. (Right) A Kekchi Indian farmer fills sacks with potatoes he has grown on land near Chelemha. Since the early 1990s, the government of Guatemala has encouraged farmers to use modern methods and grow new crops.

3 An Economy Well Positioned for Growth

GUATEMALA IS still a developing country, but one that is "well positioned for rapid economic growth over the next several years," in the words of a U.S. State Department bulletin. This seemed especially true after the signing of the Peace Accords in 1996. The United States is Guatemala's largest trading partner, providing 41 percent of Guatemala's *imports* and receiving 34 percent of its *exports*.

There are several signs that Guatemala's economy is improving. One is its increasing number of exports. In addition, investment in Guatemalan industries by other countries, such as the United States, Germany, France, Italy, Spain, and Japan, has also been speeding the country's economic progress. Finally, natural resources available for further development include rich farmland, hardwood forests, mineral deposits, and mountain rivers that can be used to provide *hydroelectric* power. On the other hand, widespread poverty, illiteracy, and health problems remain serious obstacles facing the country.

A Strong Agricultural Labor Force

Only a fraction of Guatemala's land is devoted to agriculture—about 17 percent—but the work employs half of the country's labor force. In fact, farm products amount to two-thirds of Guatemala's exports. Of those exports, coffee, which is grown on highland plantations, makes up 30 percent. Other crops raised in various parts of Guatemala include sugar cane, rubber trees, cotton, wheat, cardamom, and bananas.

In recent years, Guatemalan farmers have also been planting crops that are new to the region: lychee (a pale, sweet fruit), melon, papaya, mango, pineapple, broccoli, okra, snow peas, celery, cauliflower, asparagus, potatoes, garlic, various spices, nuts, and ornamental flowers. These are gradually making up a larger share of farm products sold outside the country. Farmers and ranchers raise beef cattle throughout Guatemala, too.

In a developing country such as Guatemala, it is not unusual for a large portion of the labor force to find work on farms and plantations, where the only requirements for a job are a strong back and willing attitude. Some Guatemalan workers live permanently on coffee plantations as *tenants*. By law, plantation owners must set aside land for raising *subsistence crops* for the tenants' use, such as corn, rice, and black beans— basic foods of most Guatemalans. Indians from the Western highlands help bring in the coffee harvest on plantations every year, because many of them do not own enough land to support themselves through farming alone.

Service Industries and Revenue

The buying and selling of agricultural products creates a lively base of trade in Guatemala. Most towns have market days, in addition to the normal commerce that takes place in larger cities having to do with finance, real estate, transportation, communication, and government. Taken as a whole, these kinds of economic activities generally come under the heading "services."

The service industries, which also include tourism, provide services rather than goods. In Guatemala, about one-third of the labor force works in the service industries, but it is the largest *revenue* generator in the country's economy. Moreover, two things indicate that the service industries will continue to grow. First, the government's control over the economy is relaxing, allowing more private businesses to develop. Second, increased tourism in recent years is creating a larger demand for hotels, restaurants, and transportation—all of which provide services.

Manufacturing and Handmade Goods

The founding in 1960 of the Central American Common Market, a union of five nations, opened other Central American countries to goods manufactured in Guatemala. Guatemalan factories produce beverages, *textiles*, cigarettes, pharmaceuticals, rubber, building materials, paper, shoes, soap, candles, plywood, petroleum, and tires. Import *duties* on

goods coming into Guatemala from its neighbors remain low, too—between 0 and 15 percent. Cheap labor and low taxes make Guatemala an attractive location for importing machine parts from the United States, which are assembled and then re-exported back to North America.

About 15 percent of the labor force is engaged in manufacturing and industry, although that figure includes the number of people working in *cottage industries*, or the home-based production of goods. Many families, especially in those areas favored by tourists, make Indian handicrafts for sale—leather goods, pottery, clothing, blankets,

A Mayan woman fashions an intricate and colorful textile. She will sell the cloth in Antigua. Indian handicrafts such as these are very popular with tourists visiting Guatemala.

Quick Facts: The Economy of Guatemala

Per capita income (2001): $3,900

Natural resources: Fisheries products, forest products, mined minerals: antimony, gold, nickel, iron ore, and lead.

Industry (20 percent of GDP*): Sugar, textiles and clothing, furniture, chemicals, petroleum, metals, and rubber.

Agriculture (23 percent of GDP): Sugar cane, corn, bananas, coffee, beans, cardamom, cattle, sheep, pigs, and chickens.

Services (57 percent of GDP): tourism and government services.

Foreign trade (2001): Exports—$2.4 billion: coffee, sugar, bananas, fruits and vegetables, meat, clothing, petroleum, and electricity.

Labor force, by occupation: Agriculture, 50 percent; industry, 15 percent; services, 35 percent.

Currency exchange rate (2002): 7.8 questzales = U.S. $1.

* GDP or gross domestic product—the total value of goods and services produced in a year

and wood carvings. Stalls featuring handmade items for tourists are a common sight in Guatemala City, Antigua, and a few Indian villages, such as Chichicastenango. Manufacturing has not been able to keep up with the number of people who have moved to the large cities in recent years, however, and unemployment is high.

Fishing, Forestry, and Mining

So far, lack of modern equipment has kept fishing, forestry, and mining from contributing in a major way to Guatemala's economy. Fishing fleets off both the Pacific and Caribbean coasts catch shrimp, snapper, and tuna, but the boats are small and privately owned. Likewise, the valuable hardwood trees in Guatemala—mahogany, balsam, and cedar—yield cabinet and furniture wood, oils, and dye. Hauling wood from remote, densely forested areas is difficult, however, because workers are forced to rely on ramps, pulleys, and other simple devices. Mining remains on a small scale—boosted or depressed by world prices and demand for Guatemala's main mineral resources: nickel, antimony, gold, iron ore, and lead.

Transportation Lags Behind

Roads provide the most important means of travel in Guatemala. The country has three major highways: the Inter-American, which runs from Mexico through the Guatemalan highlands to El Salvador; a parallel route running along the Pacific coast; and the Atlantic Highway, which starts in Guatemala City and runs to Puerto Barrios, the country's chief port, on the Caribbean. Most towns have roads leading to the national routes, but in the rainy season, they turn to mud. Fewer than 3 percent of all Guatemalans own an automobile. Many travel by bus instead. The country does have an international airport, which is located in Guatemala City.

Life on a Dollar a Day

Although official figures put the average annual income of Guatemalans at $3,900, the way in which income and wealth are distributed is tipped toward the upper end of the social scale. According to the U.S. State Department, "The wealthiest 10 percent of the population receives almost one-half of all income; the top 20 percent receives two-thirds of all income. As a result, approximately 75 percent of the population lives in poverty, and two-thirds of that number live in extreme poverty." Another source puts 53 percent of the population living on a dollar a day. "Guatemala's social indicators, such as infant mortality and illiteracy," says the State Department, "are among the worst in the hemisphere."

Outside the capital, health and education services are poor. In villages, many people suffer from respiratory illness, skin infections, and anemia due to a lack of proper vitamins in their food. Moreover, polluted soil and water cause additional suffering. The average life expectancy is only about 60 years. Schooling is required in urban areas for children ages 7 to 14, and primary education is free, but in the rural areas, less than two-thirds of the children in that age group attend school because they are needed to work at home. About one in four persons can read in the villages.

The widespread poverty, illiteracy, and lack of *infrastructure*—especially in transportation, telecommunications, and electric power—will hinder Guatemala's economic growth in the 21st century.

Young members of a poor family thresh corn in their home in Tesoro Abajo. Many families earn barely enough to sustain themselves, and disease and malnutrition are common. The problems faced by Guatemala's poverty-stricken population were compounded during the summer and fall of 2001, when a drought caused widespread food shortages.

(Opposite) The hardship of life in Guatemala is reflected in the country's artworks. This wooden sculpture of a crying child, which has tree branches for arms, is on display in Antigua. (Right) A fisherman stares down a line of riot police in the port of Champerico. In May 2001, a labor dispute between fishermen and a large shrimp company there led to violent riots.

4 Indians and Ladinos

GUATEMALANS CONSIST OF two main ethnic groups—the Indians, who account for 44 percent of the population, and the Ladinos, which is a term used to define all non-Indians, including *mestizos* (mixed Indian and Spanish ancestry), **mulattoes**, black Africans, and Europeans. Ladinos account for 56 percent of the population. Other Ladino minorities include Black Caribs or Morenos, Asians, Lebanese, and Syrians.

The Split Population

The population of Guatemala in 2000 was estimated at 12,669,576. The projected population for the year 2005 is 14,423,000, which gives Guatemala one of the highest population growth rates in Central America. Like other

33

Central American countries, Guatemala's birth and death rates are high.

Most Guatemalans live in the southern portion of the country. An estimated 40 percent of the population lived in urban areas in 2000, up from 37 percent in 1980. The most densely populated areas are Guatemala City, the surrounding areas in the highland plain, and the western part of the southern coast. Guatemala City is 10 times as large as the two other major urban centers: Quetzaltenango in the western part of the highlands and Escuintla in the Pacific coastal plain. About two-thirds of the population is rural, the majority of which are native Indians.

Guatemala has a larger proportion of Indians in its total population than any other country in Central America. Approximately half of all Guatemalans are descendents of the Maya. Although nearly 60 percent of

A group of Mayan woman get together to talk in their village, which is located in the Cuchumaten mountains, part of the western highlands of Guatemala. Indians make up a higher percentage of the population of Guatemala than any other Central American country.

the population speaks Spanish, the remainder speaks any of 20 native languages. The four main Indian language groups are Quiché, Kelchi, Cakchiquel, and Mam.

The Spaniards who settled in the lower part of the highlands in the 16th through 18th centuries divided the land among themselves and established large estates. Interbreeding between Spanish men and Indian women produced the mixed-race population of *mestizos*, which comprise most of the Ladino segment of society. Today, Ladinos own nearly 10 times the amount of land held by Indians. Beginning in the late 1980s, the Catholic Church led the way in calling for reforms to redistribute land, as well as demanding respect for human rights in Guatemala. Nevertheless, Indians continue to live in peasant villages apart from the main life of the country.

Behavior, Not Ancestry

Being a Ladino in Guatemala does not depend on a person's ancestry as much as it does on lifestyle. Although a Ladino is usually someone of mixed Spanish and Indian ancestry, a Mayan can become a Ladino by living outside the Indian community and not participating in the traditional ways. Indians are extremely poor, uneducated, and tied to the concerns of their immediate family or community. Ladinos, although many are also poor, usually have a higher standard of living than Indians and better access to health, education, jobs, and political power.

The gap between Ladinos and native Indians is partly the subject of a novel by Guatemalan author Miguel Angel Asturias. *El Señor Presidente* (1946) portrays the Guatemalan society of the 1920s, during the rule of

President Manuel Estrada Cabrera, which lasted 22 years. Asturias weaves a tale of the poor and the homeless, told against the background of the wealthy social classes of the time. Asturias is one of several Central and South American authors who have won the Nobel Prize for literature.

In the towns and cities where most Ladinos live, the social customs are European. Men and women shake hands to greet one another. Women friends sometimes exchange an affectionate kiss on the cheek. Dress is generally Western in style, simple, and casual, except in centers of business and in upscale nightclubs, where formal suits and dresses are the norm. Making appointments well in advance is important among Guatemalan professionals. They pride themselves on being punctual, which is perhaps another way they distinguish themselves from Indians.

There are other minorities in Guatemala, the largest of which is the Black Caribs. Slavery was abolished in Guatemala in 1824. The freed black slaves, most of whom were taken from the Caribbean islands, soon mixed with the Indian and Spanish population. Today, they live mostly in the Caribbean lowlands.

Creoles, or Guatemalans of pure European descent, make-up about one percent of the population.

Education in Guatemala

Schooling begins in Guatemala when a child is four years old. The first year is spent in preschool, followed by kindergarten and primary grades, elementary (six years), and finally secondary school (high school), generally for five years.

Quick Facts: The People of Guatemala

Population: 12,669,576

Ethnic groups: *Mestizo* (mixed Indian-Spanish—in local Spanish called Ladino), approximately 56 percent; Indian or predominantly Indian, approximately 44 percent.

Age structure:
0–14 years: 42 percent
15–64 years: 54 percent
65 years and over: 4 percent

Population growth rate: 2.63 percent

Birth rate: 35.05 births/1,000 population

Infant mortality rate: 47.03 deaths/1,000 live births

Death rate: 6.92 deaths/1,000 population

Life expectancy at birth:
total population: 66.18 years
male: 63.53 years
female: 68.96 years

Total fertility rate: 4.66 children born per woman.

Religions: Roman Catholic, Protestant, traditional Mayan beliefs.

Languages: Spanish, 60 percent; Amerindian languages, 40 percent.

Literacy: 55.6 percent.

*All figures 2000 estimates, unless otherwise noted.

At the secondary school level, students are allowed to choose an area of specialty in addition to their regular classes, such as secretarial work, teaching, accounting, science, or business. After graduation, students can choose to apply to college. There are public and private schools, secular and religious, all over the country. They all share a common curriculum established by the Ministry of Education, but they vary in teaching methods and available fields of study.

Regardless, nearly half of all Guatemalans receive no formal schooling. About 10 percent complete high school, and 3 percent complete college. A little more than half of the population can read.

(Opposite) A Guatemalan girl and her mother pause in front of their simple house in the El Petén district of Guatemala. The home is constructed of sticks and straw. (Right) The remains of a much grander stone structure, called the Central Acropolis. A reminder of Guatemala's ancient Mayan civilization, it is located at Tikal National Park.

5 Two Cultures, One Country

TWO CULTURES CREATED present-day Guatemala: Spanish and native Indian. In old Antigua, for instance—the country's former colonial capital—Spanish villas from the 18th century rise above the humble cottages of surrounding Indian villages where the workers lived who built the conquerors' city. Even now, the influence of two cultures can be seen in Guatemala's clothing and art, read about in the literature, and heard in the speech and music.

A "New Dawn" for the Maya

According to ancient and sacred Mayan texts, a "new dawn" for the Maya would occur in 1987. In fact, since the signing of the Peace Accords in

1996, between the government, rural guerrilla groups, and the army, a sense of identity has resurfaced for the native Indians.

Mayan beliefs and traditional ways have lasted for centuries because the Indians tried to seal themselves off from outside interference. Indian communities deliberately kept their ways of life secret. They tried to resolve their own problems, rather than turn them over to colonial authorities. Unfortunately, the Indians' differences also gave their colonial masters excuses to abuse them as outsiders. Today, most native communities still keep themselves apart from Europeans.

One of the main rallying points for present-day Mayan culture is demanding respect for their languages. Although Spanish is the most widely spoken language, there are also more than 20 native languages used throughout Guatemala. In 1990, the Congress legally recognized the Academy of Mayan Languages. Soon, all teachers in Mayan areas will be *bilingual*, teaching Mayan children in their native tongue as well as in Spanish.

Clothing is another way Mayan Guatemalans distinguish themselves. Although Mayan men usually dress in Western clothing—except in a few parts of the country—Mayan women still tend to wear a long *corte* (skirt) and a *huipíl* (blouse). On festival days, the colorful and rich designs of embroidered tunics, capes, and skirts date back to before colonial times. There are 23 different attires for men and women, depending on the native group and region. Details of handmade garments and designs identify the wearer's group and village. Designs and colors of clothing can have religious, symbolic, or magical meanings, too.

A national concern shared by Indians and Ladinos is the importance of preserving centuries-old archeological sites. Temples and buildings erected by the Maya are considered national monuments and are protected by law. As archeologists continue to uncover remains of the once-great civilization, they work with Indian spiritual organizations to improve their understanding of Mayan culture and to examine the sites without damaging or changing them. In the same way, Spanish colonial buildings receive special attention and remain protected as symbols of another important era in Guatemala's history.

The Ladino Culture

Non-Indian, or Ladino, culture is the dominant one in Guatemala. As one writer observes, "Despite the diversity of Guatemalan culture, Ladino culture is what is taught to children in schools and predominates in the media. It is the result of conquest, as reflected in some of the most important national symbols," such as the national coat of arms,

Did You Know?

- Guatemala is a democratic republic. The capital is Guatemala City.
- Guatemala's current constitution was ratified on May 31, 1985. It was suspended May 25, 1993, but reinstated June 5, 1993.
- There are three branches of government. The executive branch is led by the president and vice president. The legislative branch includes one house of Congress with 113 seats. The judicial branch consists of 13 magistrates on the Supreme Court of Justice. The president, vice president, and members of Congress are elected by popular vote to four-year terms. Supreme Court judges are elected for a five-year term by Congress.
- Political candidates generally belong to one of two major parties, the National Centrist Union and the Christian Democratic Party. However, there are several lesser parties active in politics and elections.
- The voting age is 18, although rules about being eligible to vote have historically turned away poor, rural, and native people from the polls.

Shoppers search for bargains in the Indian Market at Solola, Guatemala.

which portrays a Spanish horseman setting out, sword in hand, to conquer the land.

The religious faith of most Ladinos is Roman Catholicism, the principal religion of Guatemala, due to the efforts of Catholic missionaries between the 16th and 19th centuries. Beginning in the 1940s, however, Evangelical and Pentecostal Christian denominations gained wide followings, too. Indians who are Catholic sometimes add practices from their pre-Christian past by worshipping local gods. Features of nature, such as hills, are believed to represent gods, and Indians pray to them, especially during planting and harvesting times. Over the centuries, Indian communities have chosen patron saints without seeking church approval. A small number of Indians follow traditional Mayan beliefs only.

Ladinos consider their cuisine another hallmark that separates them from Indians. Ladino cuisine is a blend of Spanish and Mayan foods—spicy and rich. Most meals are a combination of soups, sauces, grilled or fried meat, vegetables, beans, bread, and rice. Guatemalan coffee is available everywhere. Moreover, large towns and cities feature American, Argentinean, Chinese, German, Italian, Mexican, Spanish, and fast-food restaurants. By contrast, Indians are limited by poverty to simple fare: beans, corn, and rice, primarily.

In Guatemala City, modern shopping is available, and nightlife is popular. The capital and other major cities feature performances by the National Symphony Orchestra, several youth orchestras, chamber ensembles, and the National Folkloric Ballet, in addition to plays and musical theater productions. The music heard coming from nightclubs and discotheques on weekend evenings might be contemporary rock, pop, hip-hop, jazz, or tropical rhythm groups. Even Mexican Chicano and mariachi bands play at parties and gatherings.

Some tourists filter out from the cities to the local markets, hunting for

A Guatemalan child is costumed like a bull to participate in the Conquistadors Dance, a fiesta in Chicastenango.

bargains in textiles, handicrafts, jewelry, jade carvings, leather goods, ceramics, and basketry. A few places are known for their specialties—Villa de Chinautla, San Luis Jilotepeque, and Rabinal for ceramics, for example, and Cobán for silverware. Guatemala also attracts visitors who want to see the Mayan temples at Tikal National Park or tour the enormous wildlife refuge in the Yucatán peninsula. Guatemalan guides also offer hikes in the highlands to volcanoes, whitewater rafting, sport fishing, and windsurfing.

Local festivals and religious holidays always attract a share of visitors, too.

Attending a Festival

Every town in Guatemala has at least one market day a week, set aside for trading and shopping. Market days vary from town to town. Some markets, such as those in Antigua and Chichicastenango, display items meant to catch the eye of tourists. Others, especially in small villages, are more like farmer's markets—an opportunity for the local people to stock up on supplies and visit with friends.

Each town has a patron saint. Celebrating the saint's day can last a few days, a week, or even two weeks. Vendors sell food, earrings, and trinkets in the smaller villages. Local people and visitors buy bags of *roscos* to munch on, which look like donuts and taste like stale bread, during *feria*, or fiesta time. *Saq ik*, turkey served in white sauce, is a traditional ceremonial meal served in homes during fiestas. Trucks carrying games and carnival rides plough through sometimes-muddy roads to set up amusements for fiesta-goers.

Besides having a patron saint, many towns also have other religious *icons*, usually representing other saints. These are cared for by a group of men (or women), known as a *cofradías*, elected annually by the town's people. During fiestas, the *cofradías* solemnly carries the patron saint and other religious icons through the streets in a parade, often preceded by a deafening barrage of firecrackers to frighten away evil spirits. Firecrackers are almost always part of celebrations in Guatemala. Giant strings up to 20 feet long can be purchased in most stores. Fiestas often include *toritos*—men wearing cages covered with fireworks, which explode while the *toritos* charge shrieking crowds.

All traditional fiestas include folk dancing, too, whose forms date back hundreds of years to the Spanish

Did You Know?

Independence Day is celebrated September 15. Guatemala declared its independence from Spain on that date in 1821.

conquest in the 1500s and before. Some of these dances are also rooted in traditions brought from Spain, which include Moorish and Iberian influences. Others spring from Mayan tradition; still others have African roots, brought to the Caribbean by slaves.

At fiestas, it is common to hear the national instrument, the marimba, being played. The marimba, a percussion instrument, is similar to a xylophone. Marimbas vary greatly in size, from smaller ones played by one or two players, up to instruments played by six or eight players. The first mention in history of the marimba as a native instrument appears in the *Compendium of the History of Guatemala*, written in the early 1800s by the Spanish historian Juan Domingo Juarros. He describes marimba musicians playing at the opening of the cathedral in Antigua in 1806. However, the origins of the marimba appear in an ancient Mayan manuscript, where an Indian musician plays a type of marimba made from a log. Today, marimba orchestras featuring trumpets, saxophones, banjos, and percussion instruments play in Guatemalan cities for ballroom parties and important public celebrations.

Celebrating Christian Holidays

Christian religious holidays are celebrated throughout Guatemala in large cities and small villages alike.

In the days leading up to Ash Wednesday, children decorate empty eggshells by dipping them in dyed water and filling them with confetti. Then, they seal the open end with a small piece of crepe paper. When all is ready, they sneak up behind someone and break the egg gently on the person's head, releasing a shower of confetti. On *Miercoles de Ceniza* (Ash Wednesday), the custom is to throw a pinch of flour in someone's face. All the young children go around with flour in a little plastic sack and try to surprise their friends.

By far, the most remarkable celebration in Guatemala is Easter, or *Semana Santa*, in Antigua. The festivities begin on Holy Thursday, when men dress up as Roman soldiers, mount horses, and race through the cobblestone streets and alleyways yelling in triumph, pretending to have captured Jesus. Then, early Friday morning, the families gather in front of their homes and construct detailed *alfombras*, or carpets, out of dyed sawdust. The designs are quite complex, poured through cutouts, usually of some symbol of the holy week, such as a crucifix or dove. The carpets can be as long as 40 or 50 feet and span the

Costumed musicians play a beautiful wooden marimba. This xylophone-like instrument originated in Guatemala.

entire width of the street. Families work through the morning and into the afternoon on their *alfombras*.

The processions begin sometime in the mid-afternoon. Parades of marchers start from the cathedrals of Antigua and carry massive floats. The floats, which portray scenes of the Passion of Jesus—his arrest, trial, and crucifixion—weigh hundreds of pounds and typically require 60 to 80 people to carry them. Those in the parade sing somber hymns, burn incense, and pray throughout the procession. Beneath their feet, the carpets of colorful sawdust scatter. The remainder of the weekend is spent with family and friends, who attend church together, share special meatless meals, and stroll through Antigua's streets and parks.

All Saints Day, November 1, is known as *Todos Santos* in Spanish. Families go to the local cemetery in the afternoon to decorate the graves of family members. Each person in the family brings flowers, usually armfuls of them. Then, as night comes, families light candles and eat dinner at the grave, sometimes setting aside food for the dead as a sign of remembrance. Families stay at gravesites into the early morning, talking and listening to the music of a marimba band playing at the cemetery's edge.

Did You Know?

These are the official holidays in Guatemala. Other occasions are celebrated with parties and carnivals or family get-togethers. In addition, many towns hold a *festejo*, or festival, to honor its patron saint.

- January 1—New Year's Day
- March/April—*Semana Santa* (Easter Week)
- May 1—Labor Day
- September 15—Independence Day
- November 1—All Saints Day
- December 7—*Quema del Diablo* (The Burning of the Devil)
- December 24—Christmas Eve
- December 25—Christmas Day
- December 31—New Year's Eve

A nun receives communion in Quetzaltenango during a Catholic ceremony in March 1983. The head of the Roman Catholic church, Pope John Paul II, traveled to the poverty-stricken city that month during his eight-day tour of Central America and the Caribbean. Most of the Ladino people of Guatemala are Roman Catholic, although the number of Protestant Christians is growing.

In the town of San Miguel lives the last group of traditional-speaking Mayan Indians—the Itzá. On the evening of November 2, the day after All Saints Day, they perform candle ceremonies around a few actual skulls of their ancestors. Children collect grapefruit, clean them out, carve faces and pictures into them, and then make long handles of wire. They bring their *calaveras*, or skulls, to life by lighting a candle inside them like jack o' lanterns. Then, visiting the homes of family and friends, they receive treats of sweet mango, papaya, jocote, and other local tropical fruits, and *ishpasaa*, a sweet dark drink made from corn.

A Calendar of Guatemalan Festivals

Guatemala has a large percentage of Catholics, who celebrate many of the church holidays. In addition, most large towns have patron saints. Celebrations in their names take place at different times throughout the year. Some Guatemalans of Mayan descent continue to observe special days rooted in their traditional beliefs, too.

Every town in Guatemala also has at least one market day a week devoted to trading and shopping.

January

On both **New Year's Eve** and **New Year's Day**, families gather for a midnight meal. Dancing and celebrating at local clubs is popular.

February/March/April

Townspeople wear costumes and attend outdoor fairs and dances for **Mardi Gras**. This festival is usually held in the week before Lent.

A Calendar of Guatemalan Festivals

Religious services are held during the seasons of Lent and Easter. Especially important are **Miercoles de Ceniza** (Ash Wednesday), **Holy Thursday**, **Good Friday**, and **La Semana Santa** (Easter Sunday). In the town of Antigua, residents reenact the arrest, trial, and crucifixion of Jesus Christ. They also parade through the streets, dressed in elaborate costumes and carrying religious statues. Throughout the country, Easter observances usually last a week.

July/August

Folkloric festivals are held in many towns and cities throughout Guatemala. In Antigua, live bands and traditional dances attract visitors; while in Cubulco, a fiesta of rowdy dancing and celebrating takes place the same day, usually near the end of July. During the first week of August, throughout the region of Cobán, the Paabac Indians perform traditional dances, and the Kekchis Indians wear traditional costumes and prepare special delicacies.

On August 15, a **Bank Holiday** is celebrated in Guatemala City. Residents take the day off and attend parades of marching bands.

The colonial-era Catholic church La Merced is decorated with an elaborate *alfombra* (carpet) of colored sawdust and flowers during a celebration of *Semana Santa* (Holy Week) in Antigua.

September

September 15 is Independence Day, celebrated in various ways throughout the country.

November

November 1 is **Todos Santos** (All Saints Day). On this day, families decorate the graves of family members in the afternoon.

In the small village of Santiago, located about 15 minutes from Antigua, townspeople gather together to fly giant kites with messages tied to the tails. The kites are symbols of communicating with loved ones who have passed away.

The Itza Indians blend the Catholic observance of All Saints Day with their own traditional practices of remembering ancestors. On the evening of November 2, they perform ceremonies around a few actual skulls of their ancestors. Also on that night, the children of San Francisco go door to door wearing masks and asking for treats.

December

On December 7, Guatemalans celebrate the **Burning of the Devil** with bonfires throughout the country.

Christmas preparations begin early in the month. Many large companies close in the middle of the month, giving workers two weeks or more to spend with their families. Friends and neighbors visit one another. Catholics and other Christians attend late night church services on Christmas Eve and Christmas night—December 24 and 25.

51

Recipes

Verduras En Escabeche
(Pickled Vegetables)

(Serves 6 to 8)
5 jalapeno chiles, each about 2 inches long
1 tablespoon corn oil
2 cups diagonal 1/8-inch-thick slices of carrots
1 pound cauliflower, cut into 1-inch florets
1 cup sliced onion
5 garlic cloves
1 teaspoon thyme
1 teaspoon oregano
4 bay leaves
1 teaspoon salt
1 teaspoon sugar
1 cup cider or white vinegar

Directions:
1. Fry the chile peppers in the oil for 2 minutes to soften the skins. Remove the chiles, slice them open vertically, and remove seeds and fibers. Set aside.
2. Blanch the carrots, cauliflower, onion, and garlic separately in boiling water for 2 minutes. Drain well, and mix them all together. Put them into a glass jar or stone crock.
3. Mix the thyme, oregano, bay leaves, salt, and sugar in the vinegar. Pour this over the vegetables, and mix well.
4. Allow the escabeche to marinate for a day or more before serving.

The pickles can be refrigerated or stored at room temperature in a cool place.

Picado De Rabano
(Radish Salad)

(Serves 2 to 4)
1/2 pound radishes (about 20)
12 fresh mint leaves, finely chopped
Salt to taste
1/4 cup of a mix containing 2/3 orange juice and 1/3 lemon juice

Directions:
1. Trim and thinly slice the radishes.
2. Combine sliced radishes with remaining ingredients in a bowl, and serve as a salad.

Platanos Al Horno **(Baked Plantains)**

(Serves 3)
2 tablespoons sugar
1 teaspoon ground cinnamon
2 ripe plantains with black skins
2 tablespoons butter

Directions:
1. Mix sugar and cinnamon together. Peel the plantains and split them open lengthwise, but do not cut completely through. Sprinkle them inside and out with the sugar mixture. Cut dabs of butter into the slits.
2. Coat a baking dish with butter, and add the plantains.
3. Bake in a 350° F oven 20 to 30 minutes until soft and brown. Serve warm with fresh cream and honey.

Arroz Guatemalteco
(Guatemalan-Style Rice)

(Serves 6 to 8)
2 cups long grain rice
2 tablespoons oil
1 cup mixed chopped vegetables (carrots, celery, sweet red peppers, and green peas)
Salt and pepper to taste
3 cups water
1 cup spicy tomato juice

Directions:
1. Heat oil in heavy saucepan, and add rice. Sauté lightly until rice has absorbed the oil, being careful not to let it turn brown.
2. Add mixed vegetables, salt, pepper, and tomato juice. Bring to a boil, cover, and reduce heat to low.
3. Cook for about 20 minutes until rice is tender and the liquid has been absorbed.

Frijoles Negros Volteados
(Fried Black Bean Paste)

(Serves 4)
2 cups black bean puree (canned refried black beans)
1 tablespoon oil

Directions:
1. Heat oil over moderate heat in skillet.
2. Add bean puree, and mix well with wooden spoon. Stir until puree thickens and liquid evaporates.
3. Continue to stir until mix begins to come away from skillet dryly.

Serve warm with tortillas, farmer's cheese, sour cream, bread, or with all at once.

Glossary

Bilingual—speaking two languages.

Civilian—a person who is not a member of the military.

Colonial—relating to a colony.

Continental Divide—a massive area of high ground in the interior of a continent, from either side of which a continent's river systems flow in different directions.

Convert—to change the opinions or beliefs, especially religious beliefs, of another person.

Cottage industry—a small-scale business where people mostly work at home.

Deforestation—to remove the trees from an area of land.

Duties—taxes paid on imports or exports.

Exports—goods sent out of a country for sale elsewhere.

Hydroelectric—power supplied by flowing water that turns turbines.

Icons—images that have special meaning, such as statues, medals, or paintings.

Imports—goods received into a country from outside its borders.

Infrastructure—man-made improvements, such as roads, bridges, and electric service.

Lagoons—shallow ponds leading to larger bodies of water.

Leftist guerrillas—independent bands of fighters that support a liberal, socialist, or communist political system.

Left wing—a subgroup of a larger organization that is more liberal or radical than the rest of the organization.

Mulatto—a person of mixed white and black ancestry.

Plateau—a flat area of land raised above the surrounding land.

Reform—to change and improve something by correcting faults, removing abuses, and imposing modern values.

Regime—a government that is considered to be oppressive.

Repressive—punishing people who are discontent or who disagree with the government.

Revenue—money received through commerce.

Right wing—the conservative membership of a group or political party.

Savanna—tropical grassland having no trees.

Subsistence crops—farm products such as corn, rice, or beans that are grown for the farmer's family to live on, with nothing left over to sell for profit.

Tenants—people living on land owned by someone else.

Textiles—woven cloth.

Vigilantes—independent groups of people that seek to enforce the law themselves.

Project and Report Ideas

Charts, Maps, and Posters

• Create a map showing the average rainfall in Guatemala by shading areas of the country. See Chapter 1 for figures.

• Use a chart to show the difference between a cyclone, a tornado, a monsoon, and a hurricane. Create one column for a description, one column for size and wind speed, and one column for where each type of weather occurs.

• Illustrate the way income and wealth are distributed in Guatemala as a pyramid. The U.S. State Department says, "The wealthiest 10 percent of the population receives almost one-half of all income; the top 20 percent receives two-thirds of all income. As a result, approximately 75 percent of the population lives in poverty, and two-thirds of that number live in extreme poverty."

• Create a poster called "Guatemalan Goods." Cut pictures from magazines or copy them off the Web that show the goods manufactured, grown, fished, forested, or mined in Guatemala.

• How would you design clothing that said something about you? Draw sketches. (Refer to Chapter 5 about how native Guatemalan Indians' clothing uses designs and symbols to explain who they are.)

Classroom Fiesta

• If your city, town, or village was going to have an annual festival that captured some of the best things about where you live, what should be included? In small groups, choose examples of:

> Local, popular, or traditional food
> Local or regional music (Country/Western, jazz, religious, etc.)
> Exhibitions of local crafts or hobbies (fishing, soccer, baseball, gardening, etc.)
> Displays of symbols in your area (for example, the city seal or the school mascot)
> Illustrations of native wildlife—(commonly seen plants and animals)

• Make a *calavera* (a lighted skull made from a grapefruit) as described in Chapter 5.

• Listen to marimba music.

"Cost of Living" Project

Chapter 3 points out that more than half of all Guatemalans live on a dollar a day. Figure out how much you live on a day. To calculate this, you must find out or estimate the costs of these items or resources you use every day:

Food _____ (Divide monthly cost by 30.)

Electricity _____ (Divide your parents' monthly bill by 30.)

Gas _____ (Use the same method as for electricity.)

Water _____ (Use the same method as for electricity.)

Health insurance _____ (Ask your parents for an estimate, and divide by 365 days.)

Education _____ (Find out from the principal's office how much in tax dollars is spent on each student at your school per year. Divide by 183 school days. Multiply by the number of school-age children in your family.)

Total the amount. How many people in Guatemala could support themselves on the costs tied to you each day? Show your research as a chart. Add a paragraph at the end explaining your thoughts about the results.

Reports

• Many of the serious health problems in Guatemala result from a vitamin-poor diet. Write a short report explaining the types of vitamins needed for good health and the types of illness caused when key vitamins are not present.

• Who were the Maya? Write a one-page report describing life at Tikal, for example, during the height of Mayan power.

• Write a report titled, "Rare Animals Found in the Rain Forests of Guatemala." (See Chapter 1.)

Chronology

2000 B.C.	Indian fishing communities that later become the forerunners of Maya civilization appear along the Pacific coast.
A.D. 250	Mayan temples begin to appear in the highlands.
600–900	Center of Mayan power moves to the El Petén interior lowlands.
1523	Pedro de Alvarado comes to conquer Guatemala for the king of Spain. He finds warring tribes and crushes them with his armies, including the remaining highland kingdoms of the Quiché and Cakchiquel Maya.
1542	Floods and earthquakes bury the first colonial capital city, Ciudad Vieja.
1543	Spanish colonial survivors found Antigua, the second colonial capital.
1773	Earthquakes destroy Antigua, and it is abandoned.
1776	Guatemala City, the present capital of Guatemala, is founded.
1821	Guatemala declares independence from Spain.
1898–1920	President Manuel Estrada Cabrera rules as dictator, a period of social extremes as described in Nobel Prize–winning author Miguel Angel Asturias' novel, *El Señor Presidente*.
1945	Civilian president Juan José Arévalo comes to power and tries to reform Guatemalan society.
1954	A United States–sponsored invasion leads to overthrow of Guatemala's president, Colonel Jacobo Arbenz Guzmán.
1960	Armed rebels, directed from Communist Cuba, wage guerrilla war against the government.
1968	U.S. Ambassador John Gordon Mein is assassinated by leftist guerrilla groups fighting the government.

1985   The Guatemalan government drafts a new, more democratic constitution after the U.S. cuts off further aid to the military.

1993   The government redrafts the constitution again, seeking to end conflict.

1996   The government and guerrilla groups sign Peace Accords, ending 36 years of civil war.

2000   Two-thirds of Guatemala's eligible voters elect Alfonso Portillo, who promises to continue reforming the army and protecting human rights.

2001   President Alfonso Portillo meets with U.S. President George W. Bush at the White House in July to discuss regional issues.

2002   Latin American leaders, including Alfonso Portillo, meet in Argentina for the Global Alumni Conference to discuss technological and economic issues.

Further Reading/Internet Resources

Harrison, Peter D., Colin Renfrew, and Jeremy A. Sabloff. *The Lords of Tikal: Rulers of an Ancient Maya City*. London: Thames & Hudson, 2000.

Henderson, James D. *A Reference Guide to Latin American History*. Armonk, N.Y.: M. E. Sharpe, 2000.

Mahler, Richard. *Guatemala: Adventures in Nature*. Santa Fe, N.M.: John Muir Publications, 1999.

Martin, Simon and Nikolai Grube. *Chronicle of the Maya Kings and Queens: Deciphering the Dynasties of the Ancient Maya*. London: Thames & Hudson, 2000.

O'Kane, Trish. *Guatemala: A Guide to the People, Politics, and Culture*. New York: Interlink Books, 1999.

Silverstone, Michael, and Charlotte Bunch. *Rigoberta Menchu: Defending Human Rights in Guatemala*. New York: Feminist Press, 1999.

Woodward, Ralph Lee Jr. *Central America: A Nation Divided*, 3rd ed. New York: Oxford University Press, 1999.

History and Politics

http://www.newswatch.guatemala.org/
http://www.worldskip.com/guatemala/
http://www.cia.gov/cia/publications/factbook/geos/gt.html

Economy

http://www.quetzalnet.com/
http://www.fundesa.guatemala.org/
http://www.gnofn.org/~fundesa/

Tourism

http://www.fundesa.guatemala.org/Bureau/og&c.html
http://www.fundesa.guatemala.org/GAgil/GAgil.html
http://www.lonelyplanet.com/destinations/central_america/guatemala/

**U.S. Department of Commerce
International Trade Administration**
Trade Information Center
14th & Constitution, NW
Washington, DC 20230
(800) USA-TRADE
Web: http://www.ita.doc.gov

**American Chamber of Commerce in
Guatemala**
6a, Avenida 14-77, Zona 10
Apartado Postal 832
Guatemala City, Guatemala
(502) 366-4822
(502) 366-4716
E-mail: guamcham@ns.guate.net

**Caribbean/Latin American Action
(C/LAA)**
1818 N Street, NW, Suite 310
Washington, DC 20036
(202) 466-7464

**Guatemala Human Rights
Commission/USA**
3321 12th Street NE
Washington, DC 20017
(202) 529-6599
Web: http://www.ghrc-usa.org
E-mail: ghrc-usa@ghrc-usa.org

Embassy of Guatemala
2220 R Street NW
Washington, DC 20009
(202) 745-4952
Web: http://www.guatemala-
embassy.org/eg0101.asp
E-mail: info@embassy-guatemala.org

Index

Index/Picture Credits

Contributors

Senior Consulting Editor **James D. Henderson** is professor of international studies at Coastal Carolina University. He is the author of *Conservative Thought in Twentieth Century Latin America: The Ideals of Laureano Gómez* (1988; Spanish edition *Las ideas de Laureano Gómez* published in 1985); *When Colombia Bled: A History of the Violence in Tolima* (1985; Spanish edition *Cuando Colombia se desangró, una historia de la Violencia en metrópoli y provincia*, 1984); and co-author of *A Reference Guide to Latin American History* (2000) and *Ten Notable Women of Latin America* (1978).

Mr. Henderson earned a bachelors degree in history from Centenary College of Louisiana, and a masters degree in history from the University of Arizona. He then spent three years in the Peace Corps, serving in Colombia, before earning his doctorate in Latin American history in 1972 at Texas Christian University.

Charles J. Shields, the author of all eight books in the Discovering Central America series, lives in Homewood, a suburb of Chicago, with his wife Guadalupe, an elementary-school principal. He has a degree in history from the University of Illinois in Urbana-Champaign, and was chairman of the English department and the guidance department at Homewood-Flossmoor High School in Flossmoor, Illinois.

DATE DUE

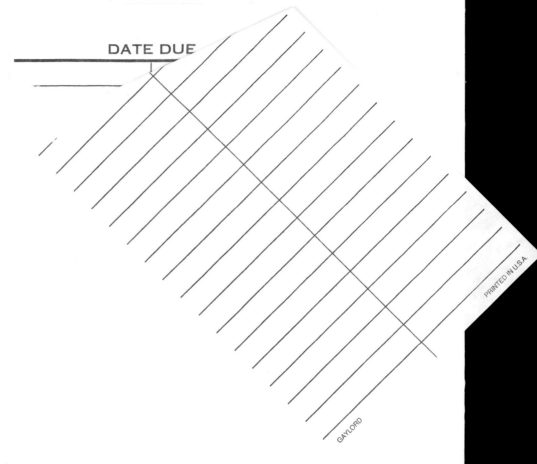

GAYLORD

PRINTED IN U.S.A.